The Power of Perseverance

A Poetic Journey of Introspection

To:

Congratulations on this momentous occasion! As you embark on the next chapter of your life, we wanted to give you a gift that will inspire and guide you for years.

Inside this book of poems, you'll find timeless messages of hope, grit, and perseverance that resonate with you as you navigate the challenges and opportunities ahead. We hope this book provides inspiration and guidance, reminding you that you can achieve great things.

We're so proud of all you've accomplished so far, and we can't wait to see all you'll achieve in the years to come. Congratulations again, and we hope you enjoy this gift!

Love,

"Pathways to Perseverance"

Amidst the robes and caps of black,
The graduates all gather back,
To hear the words of those who've come,
Before them on this long journey.

In Wallace's "This is Water,"
To Jobs' "Stay Hungry, Stay Foolish,"
Their messages of hope and grit,
Are ones that we can all cherish.

Rowling spoke of failure's power,
And how imagination flowers,
Adichie urged for gender parity,
And Sandberg called for diversity.

Brown reminded us to be accurate,
Gaiman said, "Make good art" anew,
While Zakaria praised the liberal arts,
For shaping minds and sharpening hearts.

These words of wisdom are timeless, authentic,
Are ones that we can all pursue,
As we embark on our quest,
To make our world a little less stressed.

So, here's to you, graduates all,
We hope your future will enthrall,
And as you journey through your days,
May you always find your authentic ways.

Note from the Author

Dear Graduates,

Today marks a momentous occasion in your lives. As you move on from this chapter, I want to share some wisdom from some of the greatest commencement speeches ever.

David Foster Wallace once said, "This is water." He meant that it's easy to get caught up in the routines and challenges of everyday life and lose sight of the bigger picture. But by remaining aware and present now, we can find meaning and purpose in even the most mundane tasks.
Steve Jobs urged us to "stay hungry, stay foolish." He reminded us that our passions and curiosities fuel us and that we should never stop pursuing our dreams and taking risks, even if it means being slightly foolish.

J.K. Rowling spoke about the importance of failure and imagination. She reminded us that despite setbacks and failures, we could dream and imagine new possibilities that ultimately drive us forward.

Chimamanda Ngozi Adichie spoke about the need for gender equality and the importance of inclusivity. She reminded us that everyone has the power to make a difference and that it's up to each of us to work toward a more just and equitable society.

Brené Brown spoke about the power of vulnerability and authenticity. She reminded us that our willingness to be open and honest with ourselves and others allows us to connect more deeply and meaningfully with the world around us.

Neil Gaiman encouraged us to "make good art." He reminded us that creating and expressing ourselves is vital to being human and that we should always remember the joy and wonder of making something beautiful.

Sheryl Sandberg spoke about the importance of women's leadership and diversity. She reminded us that we could only progress and create a better world for everyone by including diverse perspectives and voices.

And finally, Fareed Zakaria defended the liberal arts and their role in cultivating critical thinking and a broad perspective on the world. He reminded us that we could think deeply and engage with complex ideas that ultimately lead to innovation and progress.

So, as you move forward from this day, remember these lessons from some of the greatest minds of our time. Remember to stay aware and present, to follow your passions and take risks, to embrace failure and imagination, to work towards a more just and equitable world, to be vulnerable and authentic, to make good art, to celebrate diversity, and to engage deeply with the world around you.

Congratulations, graduates, and good luck on your journey ahead.

"The Power of Perseverance: A Poetic Journey of Introspection"

It is a collection of poems exploring the human experience's beauty and complexity. Through the power of words, these poems capture the moments that shape our lives, from joys and triumphs to struggles and setbacks. Each poem in this collection invites readers to embrace the present moment and find meaning and purpose in their lives. Whether you seek inspiration, solace, or simply a moment of reflection, these poems offer a thoughtful and thought-provoking journey through the highs and lows of life. So, join us on this journey of self-discovery and embrace the beauty and richness of life. May these poems inspire you to live fully, embrace your moments, and find your place in the world.

Table of Content

Introduction

As the author of this book, I started with some of the greatest commencement speeches because, at the time, I was thinking of a gift I could put together that would be a lasting gift for children, friends, and others to come. Based on that, I started with the collection of poems and how I would preface those with some of the greatest speeches I had read, and that resonated with the lyrics and ultimately led to the book's title.

The lessons such as "This is Water" by David Foster Wallace were given in 2005 at Kenyon College and have been widely regarded as one of the greatest commencement speeches ever. In the speech, Wallace talks about the importance of being aware of one's surroundings and the challenges of living in the modern world.

"Stay Hungry, Stay Foolish" by Steve Jobs - This speech was given in 2005 at Stanford University and has become one of the most famous commencement speeches ever. In the speech, Jobs talks about his life experiences and the importance of following one's passion.

"The Fringe Benefits of Failure and the Importance of Imagination" by J.K. Rowling - This speech was given in 2008 at Harvard University and has been widely praised for its wisdom and insight. Rowling talks about the importance of failure and imagination in achieving success in the speech.

"We Should All Be Feminists" by Chimamanda Ngozi Adichie - This speech was given in 2015 at Wellesley College and has been widely praised for its powerful message. In the speech, Adichie talks about the importance of gender equality and the need for everyone to work towards achieving it.

"The Power of Vulnerability" by Brené Brown - This speech was given in 2013 at the University of Houston and has been praised for its powerful message about the importance of vulnerability and authenticity in our lives.

"Make Good Art" by Neil Gaiman - This speech was given in 2012 at the University of the Arts in Philadelphia and has become a classic among artists and creatives. In the speech, Gaiman talks about the importance of perseverance and making art for its own sake.

"A Truly Global Endeavor" by Sheryl Sandberg - This speech was given in 2016 at Tsinghua University in China and has been praised for its insight into women's challenges in the workplace. In the speech, Sandberg talks about the importance of women's leadership and the need for greater diversity in all fields.

"In Defense of the Liberal Arts" by Fareed Zakaria - This speech was given in 2014 at Sarah Lawrence College and has been praised for its defense of the liberal arts in an era of increasing specialization. In the speech, Zakaria argues that the liberal arts are essential for developing critical thinking skills and a broad perspective on the world.

As we navigate the twists and turns of our personal and professional paths, we often encounter moments of doubt and uncertainty. But in these moments, perseverance becomes a guiding force, helping us rise above adversity and reach our goals. So come, take a journey with me, and let us discover the power of perseverance together. Reflect on the presented themes and messages as you read this book of poems. The struggles and triumphs of others are also reflected in these poems. As you reflect on the verses and your own experiences, I hope you will find inspiration and guidance for your journey of self-improvement and growth.

Through the words of these poems, I hope to inspire and encourage you to never give up on your dreams, no matter how difficult the journey may seem. May they remind us that we can conquer any obstacle and succeed in all aspects of our lives with strength, resilience, and a little introspection. Managing your career has become more critical than ever in today's fast-paced business world. With companies focused on shareholder returns and external competitive pressures, individuals must take sole responsibility for their career success. The traditional models of company security, automated career management, and traditional reward systems are becoming extinct. The shift towards flatter organizational structures and the changing employment market has created a need for diverse career paths and a talent portfolio capable of making various career moves.

This book of poetry is a collection of poems that explore the challenges and opportunities of managing your career in today's business world. Each poem reflects the struggles and triumphs that individuals face in their careers. They also provide insights and possible solutions to the talent concerns of employees and leaders.

The poems rhyme to provide a unique perspective on career management challenges. They are also designed to inspire readers to take positive actions toward building their talent portfolio.

As leaders, we must review the methods and processes we use to manage talent. We must update our leadership skills and abilities to align with the needs of managing talent in the 21st century. By understanding the market's demand for skills and abilities within our talent portfolio, we can achieve continued success in our careers.

This book is for persons interested in motivation and inspiration that educates and entertains the mind. It is excellent for those exiting college and joining the workforce. Or those in management and leadership positions and those looking to improve their career prospects. It serves as a reminder of the importance of self-awareness, self-reflection, and taking responsibility for our career development. As we navigate the modern workplace, it's essential to understand the different perspectives and experiences of the various generations that make up the workforce. Each group brings unique skills, values, and challenges from the Silent Generation to Gen Z.

Let's take this journey together and discover the power of career and business poetry in managing our professional growth and success.

One major issue that affects all generations is the importance of work culture. A positive work culture can foster creativity, productivity, and employee satisfaction. The foundation sets the environment's tone and defines how employees interact and work together. A healthy culture leads to loyalty, a sense of belonging, and employee motivation. This, in turn, helps to achieve the company's vision and goals.

Another vital aspect is diversity in the workplace. A diverse workforce brings different perspectives, ideas, and experiences to the table, which leads to innovation and creativity. It creates a more inclusive environment and provides a better understanding of different cultures and backgrounds.

The challenges that each generation faces in the workplace are also unique. The Silent Generation may face challenges related to age discrimination, while Boomers may struggle with adjusting to new technologies. Gen X may feel stuck between the older and younger generations, and millennials may need help finding a work-life balance. Gen Z may need help finding their place in the workforce and being taken seriously.

But despite these challenges, each generation can contribute to the success of a business. The Silent Generation brings experience and wisdom, Boomers bring hard work and dedication, Gen X brings adaptability and resilience, millennials bring fresh ideas and tech-savviness, and Gen Z brings drive and ambition. By understanding and valuing the contributions of each generation and fostering a positive work culture and a diverse workforce, businesses can achieve success and create a better future for all.

In summary, each generation brings unique strengths and challenges to the workplace, and it's essential to understand and value their contributions. Positive work culture and diversity in the workplace are critical to a business's success and growth. By fostering a positive and inclusive environment, companies can ensure that all employees can thrive and reach their full potential. In this section of the book, the poems display the prevailing sentiment of general populations of individuals in each generation during this book's development.

In this book, I invite you to join me on a poetic journey of introspection as we explore the power of perseverance in our careers and life. Each poem in this collection reflects the challenges we face, the obstacles we overcome, and the lessons we learn.

Let's get started,

The traditional natural and progressive period of change has given way to an era of obligatory change. The substantial changes in the employment market have negatively and positively affected workers. No longer can employees assume that they are guaranteed a position or that they will receive desired salary increases and promotions by doing the same thing year after year. The shift towards flatter organizational structures has created a need for varied career paths for employees, with no predetermined career progression or reward systems.

In today's employment market, workers must have a talent portfolio that can make diverse career moves. The employee's talents must align with the skills the employment market requires to be positioned for continued employability with current or future organizations. To build a talent portfolio, workers must find the necessary resources to manage their careers. They must also capitalize on all available learning resources through their employer, education, online learning, and community resources.

Leaders, managers, and organizations are tasked with helping employees adjust to the new talent market requirements. As a leader, it is essential to realize the monumental task that leaders and managers have in 21st-century organizations. We are tasked with managing talent through non-traditional models. Management now requires structures that include coaching based on the employee's needs rather than the control of the task. The coaching needs of the employee are paramount to achieving a talent balance with the company's core competencies.

Coaching is imperative to the achievement of organizational growth and career substance.

As a leader, it is also essential to understand the views and perceptions of employees regarding talent concerns. Employee views and perceptions can be expressed through poetic rhyme to provide insight and possible solutions. Employees can achieve future career success by understanding the market's need for skills and abilities within their talent portfolio. As leaders, we must review the methods and processes we use to manage talent and update our leadership skills and abilities to equate to those needed for managing talent instead of operations.

The new talent market demands a new way of thinking about career management and leadership. Workers must have a talent portfolio capable of making diverse career moves, and leaders must have the necessary skills and abilities to manage talent through non-traditional models. It is essential for both employees and leaders to capitalize on all available learning resources and to understand the views and perceptions of employees regarding talent concerns. By doing so, we can achieve organizational growth and career substance in a constantly changing and dynamic market.

In addition, we have also explored the concept of continuous learning and the importance of building a talent portfolio in today's ever-changing employment market. We have highlighted the need for employees to be adaptable and to continuously develop their skills to stay competitive in the job market. We have also emphasized the role of leaders, managers, and organizations in helping employees adjust to the new talent market requirements.

Throughout this book, we have used poetry as a tool for introspection and reflection. The poetry has provided a unique perspective on various topics related to self-discovery, career, and community. We hope the poetry has resonated with you and given you pause for introspection and reflection. We have included various resources at the end of the book to help you continue your journey of self-discovery and career development. We encourage you to use these resources and build your talent portfolio. We would love to hear your thoughts about the book and how it has impacted you. Please get in touch with us at the publisher or through the information provided. We hope this book has been a valuable resource for you and helped you on your self-discovery and career development journey.

"Embrace Change"

This poem encourages embracing change and taking control of one's future. It encourages readers to see the possibilities and opportunities of change and approach them openly and enthusiastically. The poem also emphasizes the importance of recharging, spending time with loved ones, and pursuing passions. Ultimately, it reminds us that every day is an opportunity to create memories and live life to the fullest.

The future is ours to shape,
A canvas ready to create.
Let's embrace the change that's here,
And ignite growth, make it clear.

Weekends are a time to recharge,
A moment to slow down and discharge.
To spend time with loved ones near,
Or pursue a passion, no longer fear.

So, let's make the most of every day,
Live life to the fullest in every way.
Create memories that will last,
A story to tell, an extended life.

The possibilities are endless, it's true,
With each sunrise, a fresh start anew.
So, let's embrace this change with open arms,
And shape the future with all our charms.

"The Power of Perseverance"

Amidst the twists and turns of life's terrain,
The journey to success is not in vain,
For those who brave the wind and rain,
With perseverance, they shall attain.

Obstacles may rise to the sky,
Challenges that seem to multiply,
But with unwavering strength inside,
Perseverance will be their guide.

In moments of despair and doubt,
When hope seems like it's run out,
Perseverance will help them surmount,
And lift them from within, no longer without.

For every setback, they may face,
A lesson to learn, a step to retrace,
Perseverance in their hearts and their pace,
To push them forward to the finish line race.

With every step and every breath,
They march forward beyond life's breadth,
Perseverance is a force that never leaves,
A journey of introspection, they have kept.

"The Jonrowe Journey"

Verse 1:
A journey starts with a single step.
And a spark of curiosity in our hearts
We set out to explore, to discover.
To seek knowledge and uncover the uniqueness within.

Chorus:
The Jonrowe journey, a path to tread
Filled with lessons, growth, and bread.
We'll learn and grow; we'll reach new heights.
With open minds and hearts filled with lights

Verse 2:
From the past to the present, we'll delve.
Into the stories and lessons they tell.
We'll look at the future with hope and dreams,
And the plans and schemes for what it brings.

Chorus:
The Jonrowe journey, a path to tread
Filled with lessons, growth, and bread.
We'll learn and grow; we'll reach new heights.
With open minds and hearts filled with lights.

Verse 3:
We'll explore the world and the people in it
And how we all fit.
We'll learn about ourselves and our place,
In this world and human experiences.

Chorus:
The Jonrowe journey, a path to tread
Filled with lessons, growth, and bread.
We'll learn and grow; we'll reach new heights.
With open minds and hearts filled with lights

Outro:
So, come along, and join us on this ride.
We'll explore, learn, and never hide.
The Jonrowe journey is a path to take.
With each step, we'll learn, grow,
and make the most of our talents and skills to
embark on each journey we partake in.

"Conquering Time: A Journey of Grit and Management"

Preserve through time with grit and care,
Manage each moment with a mindful air.

Stay focused on the task at hand,
And make the most of every stand.
With determination in every stride,
Conquer the obstacles that come in sight.

Push forward with relentless drive,
And strive for the goal that you desire.

Be mindful of the minutes that slip,
And always keep them from giving you a dip.

Use each second wisely and honestly,
To make the most of all you do.

And when the day is done and through,
Reflect on all you've accomplished too.

Take pride in your hard work and might,
For it is this that will keep you bright.

So, hold on tight to your passion's fire,
And never let it be put out by tire.

Preserve through time with grit and grace,
And success will always be in place.

"You're Secret Sauce"

Within each of us lies a secret sauce,
A blend of values, strategies, and experience,
That guides us through life's ups and downs,
And helps us make sense of the chaos and routine.

In the craziness of work and the mundane,
We each find our way to navigate,
Some through discipline and others through purpose,
Finding what feels right to help us create.

In relationships, we have our unique approaches,
Some prize honesty, others empathy, and understanding,
But what matters most is what we value,
And the connections that we are demanding.

As we learn and grow, we find our path,
Some through curiosity, others through discipline,
But the secret sauce that we each have within,
It is what helps us succeed and win.

And as parents, we each have our style,
Some through structure, others through love and affection,
But what matters most is what we believe,
And how we guide our children to perfection.

So, embrace your secret sauce, and let it guide you,
In all of life's joys and struggles, let it inspire you,
For it is the unique blend that makes you, you,
And it will help you be your most accurate and best you.

"From Ashes to Beauty: A Journey of Triumph"

Rise from the ashes of what once was lost,
Embrace the journey with courage at a cost,
For you were forged in the fire of life's pain,
And tempered by love, like diamonds in the rain.

You've fought the battles and faced the unknown,
With grace and dignity, never feeling alone,
For you know the strength that lies within your heart,
The courage to stand and make a brand-new start.

So don't look back with tears in your eyes,
The journey ahead holds the most fabulous prize,
With each step you take, you'll grow, and you'll shine,
And your spirit will soar on the winds of time.

And when you reach the end of your long hard road,
You'll stand tall and proud, with a heart overflowing,
For you'll have become the person you were meant to be,
With love and light, shining bright for all to see.

So, rise, my friend, and seize the day,
For you are the master of your way,
With hope and courage, you'll make your dreams come true,
And bring tears to our eyes with the beauty of you.

"Every Sunrise, A New Start"

This poem encourages embracing change and taking advantage of the present moment. It highlights that the future is ours to shape and that we should approach it with open arms and a willingness to create and grow. The poem also emphasizes the importance of recharging and pursuing one's passions, particularly on weekends. Ultimately, the poem is a call to action to live life fully and make the most of every opportunity.

The future is ours to shape,
A canvas ready to create.
Let's embrace the change that's here,
And ignite growth, make it clear.

Weekends are a time to recharge,
A moment to slow down and discharge.
To spend time with loved ones near,
Or pursue a passion, no longer fear.

So, let's make the most of every day,
Live life to the fullest in every way.
Create memories that will last,
A story to tell, an extended life.

The possibilities are endless, it's true,
With each sunrise, a fresh start anew.
So, let's embrace this change with open arms,
And shape the future with all our charms.

"The Struggle for Workplace Balance"

This poem addresses why people quit their jobs and the importance of finding a workplace that values equal pay, opportunities, respect, flexibility, benefits, and support.

Low pay and lack of advancement,
Feeling disrespected, with no enhancement.
Childcare struggles, inflexible hours,
Benefits could be improved, with more power.

These are the reasons we leave our jobs,
We were searching for something that aligns with our lobs.
A balance of pay, respect, and growth,
And a workplace that values us both.

But until we find that perfect fit,
We'll continue to quit and admit,
That the current state of the workforce,
Needs a change, of course.

So, let's strive for better for all,
Equal pay, opportunities, and a respectful call,
Flexibility, benefits, and support for all,
They stand tall for a happier workforce—the name for this poem.

"The Emotions of Job Searching"

It is a poem that addresses the concept of rage-applying and the importance of considering the long-term effects of impulsive job searching. It also highlights the importance of recognizing one's worth and making informed decisions when looking for a job.

Rage-applying, a new term in play,
A sign of frustration and wanting to stray.
From a job that doesn't fulfill or inspire,
But leaves us feeling like we're stuck in a mire.

We know our worth, and we won't settle for less,
But in the heat of the moment, we can't help but express,
Our anger and frustration, in the form of a new job search,
But is it the best move? Is it worth the lurch?

When we're doing anything out of rage,
We're not thinking long-term; it's all in our favor,
Emotions are high, and rational thought low,
We may regret it when we're ready to go.

So, let's take a breath and think it through,
Is this job for you and me?
Let's weigh the pros and cons and make a sound choice,
And know that our worth will always rejoice. Name for this poem.

"The Millennial Mindset"

This poem explores the perspective and characteristics of the millennial generation, who are often seen as tech-savvy and driven by change, and the importance of understanding and not judging them for their unique ways of thinking and perspective on the world.

A generation of tech and change,
Millennials are often seen as strange.
With smartphones in hand and eyes on screens,
They navigate a world not yet seen.

They march for causes and speak their mind,
They're not afraid to be unkind,
To systems that don't serve them well,
And strive for a world that's not so hell.

They value experiences over things,
And prioritize their spread wings,
They're not afraid to break the mold,
And pave a path that needs to be told.

They're a diverse group with different views,
But all united in their quest for news,
Of a better world for all to share,
And a future that's bright and fair.

So, let's not judge them for their ways,
They're just a generation in different phases,
And who knows, they might be surprised,
And change the world before our eyes.

"The Power of Work Culture"

It is a poem highlighting the importance of positive work culture in fostering success, happiness, and innovation among employees and how it can lead to employee loyalty and investment in the company's goals and vision.

Work culture, the backbone of a business,
A foundation for success and happiness.
It sets the tone and defines the way,
For employees to work and to play.

It's the values, the beliefs,
That shapes the environment and the reliefs.
It's the way we treat each other,
And the way we work together.

A positive culture leads to loyalty,
And a sense of belonging for all to see.
It fosters creativity and innovation,
And sets the stage for growth and liberation.

A healthy culture brings out the best,
In employees, and helps them to invest,
In the company's goals and the company's vision,
For a better future, with a clear decision.

So, let's strive for a positive culture,
That brings out the best in every creature.
For a better workplace and better success,
It is built on a foundation of happiness.

"A Tapestry of Diversity"

It is a poem highlighting the importance of diversity in the workplace and how it enriches the work environment, brings new perspectives, ideas, and experiences, and makes the workplace stronger and more inclusive. The title also references the metaphor of a tapestry, created by weaving different colors and threads together to create a beautiful and intricate whole.

Diversity in the workplace, a tapestry of hue,
A blend of cultures, backgrounds, and views.
Different languages and different ways,
But united in our common goal, to amaze.

Different perspectives and other ideas,
Bring innovation and solutions to the seers.
Diversity of thought and diversity of skill,
Make the workplace stronger and more still.

Different experiences and different paths,
Enrich the workplace and leave lasting marks.
A diversity of ages and a variety of genders,
Make the workplace more inclusive and tenders.

Diversity in the workplace is not a choice,
But a necessity to hear different voices.
It's not about being the same but about valuing the differences,
That makes us unique and makes us more efficient.

So, let's embrace diversity in all its forms,
For a better workplace and a brighter norm.
A tapestry of colors and a tapestry of ideas,
Make the workplace a beautiful place to be.

"The Intergenerational Workforce"

It is a poem highlighting the diversity of the five generations in the workplace and their unique perspectives, skills, and contributions to the workforce. The title emphasizes the idea of different generations working together and how this intergenerational dynamic can lead to a better workplace and a brighter future.

Five generations, in the workplace, we see,
Each one with their reality.

The Silent Generation, hardworking and trustworthy,
Their experience is an asset to pursue.

Boomers, the backbone of our nation's tide,
Their hard work, and pride, always abide.

Gen X, the bridge between the old and new,
Their perspective is fresh and unique to pursue.

Millennials, a generation of change and tech,
Their ideas, fresh and unexpected, to check.

Gen Z, the future of our society,
Their potential and drive for a better world to be.

Together, we all bring something to the table,
Diverse perspectives and skills to enable.
A better future for all to share,
With cooperation and collaboration, we'll be there.

So, let's embrace the differences and learn,
For a better workplace and a brighter turn.
Five generations, working side by side,
Building a better world with pride.

"The Millennial Mindset"

This poem explores the perspective and characteristics of the millennial generation, who are often seen as tech-savvy and driven by change, and the importance of understanding and not judging them for their unique ways of thinking and perspective on the world.

A generation of tech and change,
Millennials are often seen as strange.
With smartphones in hand and eyes on screens,
They navigate a world not yet seen.

They march for causes and speak their mind,
They're not afraid to be unkind,
To systems that don't serve them well,
And strive for a world that's not so hell.

They value experiences over things,
And prioritize their spread wings,
They're not afraid to break the mold,
And pave a path that has yet to be told.

They're a diverse group with different views,
But all united in their quest for news,
Of a better world for all to share,
And a future that's bright and fair.

So, let's not judge them for their ways,
They're just a generation in different phases,
And who knows, they might be surprised,
And change the world before our eyes.

"The Boomers' Legacy"

Is a poem highlighting the contributions and characteristics of the Baby Boomers generation, their hard work, perseverance, and determination to make the world a better place for their children and future generations? The title also emphasizes the idea of Boomers leaving a legacy for future generations to learn from and admire.

A generation of hard work and pride,
Boomers the backbone of our nation's tide.
They've seen it all and done it too,
From civil rights to the Cold War blues.

They've built the roads and the bridges high,
They've fought for peace and reached for the sky.
They've raised families, and held down jobs,
And built a life with no time for slobs.

They've lived through changes and adapted well,
And have stories to tell and to tell.
They've seen the world and made it better,
For their children and their children's children forever.

They've faced challenges and overcome them,
With determination and a will to be done.
They're not ready to slow down yet,
And have much more to do and to set.

So, let's give thanks to the Boomers for all they've done and for all they'll do,
We should admire their generation because we need their wisdom to help us see through.
And learn from them as we move forward in the madness of the new world order with AI, ChatGPT, and Crypto establishing a new order.

"Love and Power"

The black canvas, a vast expanse,
With gold down the middle, like a dance,
A wave of riches, moving with grace,
A symbol of power in this place.

The gold glimmers in the light,
A symbol of wealth, shining so brightly,
A path to success, or so it seems,
But what lies beneath this dream?

The black surrounds a mystery untold,
A reminder of what's yet to unfold,
The balance of power, so fragile and frail,
A warning to tread with caution and scale.

The wave moves on, with the ebb and flow,
A reminder that nothing is certain, we know,
The gold may glitter, but it can also fade,
Leaving behind a life that's been played.

"Ghost Horse"

A ghostly figure, standing by his side,
A shadow of a horse, yet full and proud,
Embodying the spirit, strength, and pride,
Of independence, freedom, and the crowd.
With power and courage, he stands alone,
Enduring the winds of change and time,
His symbol, a reminder of a known,
A hero's journey, in the end, is sublime.
But what of this shadow, this ghost horse,
A reflection of the past or the future,
A reminder of the choices we endorse,
Or a warning of what we may incur.
With every step, we choose our path,
And in this journey, the ghost horse is our math.

"Courage in Black and Gold"

With brush in hand and heart full of pain,
He painted a symbol of hope and might,
A reminder of the love that was in vain,
And the courage to face the darkest night.
In black and gold, the word "courage" shines,
A beacon amid fear and doubt,
A call to rise above the most challenging times,
And to never back down or back out.
For when the world is dark and full of strife,
We must look within to find the light,
To summon the strength to conquer fear and life,
And to love ourselves with all our might.
For, in the end, true courage lies within,
And with it, we will conquer, we will win.

"Currency"

In shades of gold and green, a picture stands,
A symbol of our modern way of life,
Of wealth and power, wealth in many hands,
And power held by those who own the strife.
On one side, gold, a symbol of the past,
On another, cash, the present flow,
And on the last, crypto, the future cast,
A tale of what is yet to come, we know.
But what does this picture indeed mean,
Is it a tale of greed or one of hope,
A warning of the future yet unseen,
Or a call to find a better way to cope.
For, in the end, we all must choose our fate,
And with our choices, our future we create.

"Love in Crypto"

In shades of black and green, a picture shows,
A symbol of our digital age,
Of love and technology combined,
A tale of the future on a page.
The word "love" in bold, across the screen,
A reminder of what truly matters,
In a world where all is not as it seems,
And where the future often shatters.
But what does this picture honestly say,
Is it a tale of love or one of loss,
A warning of the future, come what may,
Or a call to find a way across.
For, in the end, we all must choose our fate,
And with our choices, our future we create.

"Black and Gold Wave"

In shades of black and gold, a picture seen,
A symbol of the ebb and flow of life,
Of highs and lows, of joy and sorrow keen,
And the journey through the ever-changing strife.
A wave, a metaphor for the journey,
Of life's ups and downs, in an endless tide,
A reminder that in life, we must be,
Flexible and robust, not to run and hide.
But what does this picture indeed mean,
Is it a tale of hope or one of fear,
A warning of the future, yet unseen,
Or a call to find a way out of here.
For, in the end, we all must choose our fate,
And with our choices, our future we create.

21st Century Life and Wealth

The black canvas serves as a backdrop.
For the silver paintings that come alive
Crypto, music notes, and the number one
All come together to thrive.
The hand, a symbol of human touch
Guiding the scene, an artist's brush
Crypto, a symbol of wealth and power
The music notes, a symbol of art and culture
Together they paint a picture.
Of a world where money and passion coexist
Where the love for music and the love for crypto
They are intertwined and persist.
A world where one can find success.
In both the digital and creative spheres
Where the hand of the artist guides the way
To a future full of endless cheers.

The black canvas serves as a stage.
For silver paintings to play their part
Crypto, music notes, and the number one
Each adds to the work of art.
The hand, a symbol of human touch
Guiding the scene, an artist's brush
Crypto, a symbol of wealth and power
The music notes, a symbol of art and culture
Together they paint a picture.
Of a world where money and passion coexist
Where the love for music and the love for crypto
Are intertwined and persist.

A world where one can find success.
In both the digital and creative spheres
Where the hand of the artist guides the way
To a future full of endless cheers.

The black canvas reflects the uncertainty.
Of a world in constant change
The silver paintings, a symbol of hope
Amid a modern age
Crypto, music notes, and the number one
Represent the paths we must choose.
The hand is a reminder of the power.
Of the decisions we make and use
Crypto, a symbol of the digital age
Where wealth can be gained and lost in a day or moment
The music notes, a symbol of culture
And the beauty it can engross.
Together they paint a picture.
Of a world that is both complex and vast
A world where we must navigate.
The challenges and opportunities of the past
A world where one can find success.
In both the digital and creative spheres
Where the hand of the artist guides the way
To a future full of endless cheers.

"Courage in Black and Gold"

Amidst the darkness of the pandemic,
A starving artist sat alone,
His heart was heavy with the loss of love,
A tone consumed his mind.
He picked up his brush and began to paint,
His emotions flowing through the strokes,
The black and gold colors on the canvas,
Reflecting the sadness in his heart and hopes.
The word "courage" he wrote across the center,
A reminder to himself to be strong,
To persevere through the pain and sorrow,
And to find a way to move on.
He painted through the night,
His heart and soul are on the line,
And as the sun rose,
He knew he would be fine.
He stepped back and viewed his work,
A symbol of his inner strength,
A reminder that in the darkest times,
Courage is what will help us to move on and length.
This painting was his way of expressing,
The resilience and determination,
To overcome the struggles of life,
And find a way to live with passion.

"Technology Meets Currency"

It is a poem about how we value wealth and how it has evolved.

Amid wealth and power,
A picture painted, bold and true,
A glimpse of the world's obsession,
With the cash, old and new.
One-third of the canvas, golden hues,
A symbol of wealth and prestige,
A reminder of the timeless value,
Of the metal, forever blessed.
Another third, cash in hand,
A hundred-dollar bills, crisp and new,
A symbol of tangible wealth,
That we all strive to pursue.
And the final third, a digital world,
Cryptocurrency, the new age,
A sign of the ever-evolving,
Financial landscape, free from rage.
Together they tell a story,
In our constant search for wealth,
A reminder of the different paths,
That we all pursue to gain and to be in health.

"Love and Crypto"

In a world of numbers and code,
Where wealth is measured in bits and bytes,
A message emerged, simple and bold,
Love is spelled out in neon lights.

The artist, a crypto trader,
Who had made his fortune online,
He decided to use his wealth,
To spread a divine message.

He painted the word with great care,
Embedding it in a sea of crypto,
This a reminder that in this digital world,
Love still has a place to grow.

The painting quickly went viral,
Shared and liked by many,
A beacon of hope in a world,
Where greed and wealth can be plenty.

And so, the artist's message,
Of love and hope persists,
This a reminder that in a world of crypto,
Love is what truly exists.

Is it Gold, Cash, or Crypto?

A symbol of wealth and power,
Or so I am told.
But as I look closer,
I see the cash in hand,
A hundred-dollar bills,
A real demand.
And then, in the corner,
In the digital world,
Cryptocurrency,
A new form of unfurled.
Together they tell a story,
Of our constant greed,
A never-ending cycle,
Of insatiable need.
Gold, cash, and crypto,
All symbols of our desire,
A never-ending pursuit,
Of wealth, forever higher.
But at what cost, I wonder,
As I gaze upon this scene,
For, in the end, all that glitters,
It is only sometimes what it seems.

"AI and ChatGPT"

A world of AI, a world of change,
A new set of skills to learn and arrange.
Communication, critical thinking, and adaptability,
The keys to thriving in this new reality.
Data analysis, technical proficiency,
To understand and work with the latest efficiency.
Creativity, thinking outside the box,
And generate new ideas to outsmart the clock.
Empathy and emotional intelligence,
To connect with humans and make sense.
A willingness to learn and evolve,
To keep up with the rapid technological revolve.
In this new world, where AI and ChatGPT,
It will play a significant role in every set.
It's not about replacing human skills,
But about augmenting them and finding new thrills.
So, let's embrace the future with open hearts,
And hone our skills for a brighter start.
In a world of AI and ChatGPT,
There's an endless opportunity for all to be set and find ways to win, win, win.

"My Career"

My career is mine to mold and shape,
To build and grow, to set the pace,
With the skills and talents I possess,
I strive to reach success, nonetheless.

I take control of my fate,
I manage my career before it's too late,
I invest in education and training,
To build my talent and keep it sustaining.

I seek out mentors and coaches,
To guide me through my career approaches,
I network and build connections,
To open doors for new dimensions.

I stay informed of industry trends,
And adapt my skills to meet the demands,
I take calculated risks and innovate,
To stay ahead and to differentiate.

I balance my work and personal life,
To maintain a healthy, motivated mind,
I strive for growth and to achieve,
To make the most of my career, and to believe.

A career is not just a job to sustain,
But a path to growth, progress, gain,
So, I'll take charge and make it mine,
To reach success and to truly shine.

"Building Social Capital"

Social capital, a wealth untold,
A network of connections, a treasure to hold,
It's not just about money or fame,
But the relationships and connections we claim.

It's the trust and support of our peers,
The mentorship and guidance that helps us persevere,
It's the doors that open, the opportunities gained,
The support and resources that help us maintain.

It's the reputation we build, the trust we earn,
The value we bring, the bridges we burn,
It's the sum of our interactions, the value we bring,
Social capital helps us take wing.

"The Power of Political Capital"

In politics, the game is won,
Those who hold power,
The ones who have the capital,
To make decisions in the hour.

It's not just money they possess,
But connections, friends, and sway,
They know the right people,
And can make things happen, come what may.

They have the ears of leaders,
And the trust of their peers,
They navigate the system,
With a finesse, that's sincere.

But political capital isn't just for those in office,
It's for the citizens, too,
It's the power to make a change,
And to see your views come through.

So, build your network,
And make your voice heard,
For political capital,
It is a powerful tool, unobserved.

With it, you can shape the future,
And make a difference in the world,
So, invest in it wisely,
And watch your political capital unfurl.

"The Power of the Mind"

We all possess it, this hidden gem,
A treasure trove of knowledge,
A wealth of information,
Capital of the mind.

It's the key to success,
The path to progress,
The way to innovation,
The source of excellence.

It's the knowledge we acquire,
The skills we develop,
The ideas we generate,
The creativity we unleash.

It's the foundation of our power,
The driving force of our ambition,
The fuel for our aspirations,
The engine of our drive.

It's the ability to think,
To reason, to analyze,
To understand, to learn,
To grow, to evolve.

It's the wealth that never depreciates,
The asset that never loses value,
The investment that always pays off,
The capital of the mind.

So let us nurture it,

Cultivate it,

Expand it,

And harness its power,

For it is the key to our success,

Our progress,

Our innovation,

And our excellence.

"The Power of Psychological Capital"

Mental strength and resilience,
A force to be reckoned with,
Psychological capital,
A well of potential, unfurled.

Self-efficacy and hope,
Positive attitudes and zest,
The drive to overcome,
And to always do our best.

Optimism and confidence,
To face and conquer fear,
The ability to bounce back,
And to persevere.

The power of psychological capital,
A treasure to be found,
A source of strength and motivation,
To lift us off the ground.

So let us nurture and develop,
This inner resource we hold,
For the power of psychological capital,
It will help us reach our goals.

"The Strength of PsyCap"

Our minds are a treasure trove,
A well of knowledge to explore,
But it's not just facts and figures,
It's our psychological capital that triggers.

It's the belief in ourselves,
The optimism and resilience,
It's the confidence to face challenges,
And the ability to bounce back with persistence.

It's the hope that drives us forward,
The grit that keeps us going,
It's the optimism that fuels our dreams,
And the resilience that keeps them glowing.

Our psychological capital is a powerful force,
It shapes our thoughts and guides our course,
It's the foundation of our success,
And the key to unlocking our potential, no less.

So let us nurture and cultivate,
Our psychological capital, with care and grace,
For it's the key to unlocking our true selves,
And reaching new heights in every race.

"Investing in Our Human Capital"

Human capital, the value within,
A force to be reckoned with, a power to win,
It's the sum of all our skills and talents,
The knowledge and abilities that makes us vital and relevant.

It's the education and experience we acquire,
The traits and characteristics that make us aspire,
To be the best versions of ourselves,
To reach new heights and excel.

It's the passion and drive that fuels our fire,
The determination that makes us go higher,
It's the ability to adapt and change,
To overcome obstacles and to arrange.

It's potential for growth and development,
The ability to create and invent,
It's the foundation for success,
And the key to progress.

So let us nurture and invest in ourselves,
In our human capital, our worth,
For it's the foundation for success,
And the key to achieving our best.

"Reflections Within"

I look within to find my truth,
To understand my inner youth,
To see my thoughts, my fears, my dreams,
And all the things that make me beam.

I look within to find my strength,
To understand my self-length,
To see my weaknesses, my doubts, my goals,
And all the things that make me whole.

I look within to find my guide,
To understand my inner tide,
To see my values, my morals, my beliefs,
And all the things that give me relief.

I look within to find my path,
To understand my aftermath,
To see my purpose, my mission, my drive,
And all the things that keep me alive.

I look within to find my peace,
To understand my inner release,
To see my balance, my harmony, my grace,
And all the things that put a smile on my face.

So let me take this time to look within,
To understand my inner win,
Only through introspection,
Can I find true self-perfection?

"A Balance of Career and Passion:
A Poem on Finding Harmony in Life and Work"

A balance of career and passion,
A path to earning and fashion,
An 8-hour day, a steady pace,
To ease financial worries, to keep up the race.

The work may be dull, the problems minor,
But I return each day to rise above it all,
My career is not just a job to sustain,
It's a growth path to progress, to gain.

Beyond the hours, it calls to me,
To push ahead, to be all I can be,
With focus and drive, I'll rise above,
And find new opportunities to explore and love.

My passion, too, is a driving force,
It brings change, creativity, and a different source of,
It reaches beyond income to build self-worth,
And allows my talents to flourish, explore, and birth.

So let them both intertwine,
Career and passion, a balance divine,
A path to earning, a way to growth,
A journey to self-discovery, to explore, to both.

"The Intertwining of Career and Passion: A Poem on Finding Harmony and Success"

Together they form a perfect blend,
Career and passion, till the very end,
One to provide for daily needs,
The other is to feed the soul, to plant the seeds.

With passion, the heart comes alive,
With a career, the mind thrives,
They both help me to grow,
To reach new heights, to know.

With passion, I can explore,
With my career, I can soar,
They both help me to find,
My purpose, my love, my grind.

With passion, I can create,
With my career, I can innovate,
They both help me to shine,
To be the best version of mine.

So let me embrace them both,
Career and passion, a perfect oath,
To work hard and to dream,
To live a life that's fulfilling.

"The Journey of Continuous Growth and Improvement: A Poem on Embracing Change and Progress"

I can't stand still, for growth is my quest,
A decision I make each day to invest,
In knowledge, education, and new experiences,
To propel me forward to new frontiers and fences.

Change is a part of the growth process,
A push to new areas, geographies, and access,
To new perspectives, new ways of thinking,
A path to self-discovery and new beginnings.

Improvement is my desire to increase,
To discover new things, to innovate and release,
My talents, skills, and abilities,
To reach new heights, to achieve new possibilities.

Growth and improvement lead the way,
To self-sufficiency and a brighter day,
A cycle of continuous change, to extend,
To new directions across global and domestic trends.

So, let me embrace them both,
Growth and improvement, my guiding oath,
For they are my best friends,
On my journey to success, until the very end.

"The Layoff: A Poem on Learning from Setbacks, Taking Responsibility, and Moving Forward"

The layoff, a harsh reality,
A blow to all, a tragedy,
When goals are met but growth is slow,
And opportunities for team expansion, woe.

A dilemma, when the department changes,
And progress stalls, causing setbacks and pains,
Years of sweat and labor were lost in an instant,
Market share and knowledge workers, in a constant.

Unforeseen challenges for potential growth,
And expansion, leading to mergers and acquisitions, both,
Filling the gap for indolent, outdated, and disengaged,
Talent, leading to downsizing, layoffs, and poor value to be gauged.

Why didn't we see it coming, this disaster,
Leadership and management, calls for action, a master,
But what role did I play in this tragedy,
Do I not possess a shareholder or stakeholder significance query?

Nothing left now but to move on,
And in the future, to be more aware, to be strong,
To question decisions, to use my vote,
To remove substandard leaders and to promote.

Engage, employ, and absorb,
To increase the proceeds of my stakeholder and value proposition, a job.

The layoff is a reminder to be constantly aware,
To focus on organizational leaders, goals, and directions, to repair,
To ensure that my actions align with the greater good,
And to always strive, for the best outcome, as I should.

"The Harsh Lesson of Layoff:
A Poem on Embracing Change, Progress,
and Learning from Setbacks"

The layoff, a harsh lesson,
This a reminder to never become complacent,
To continually strive for growth and innovation,
And to never let complacency become a temptation.

To question decisions and to speak up when wrong,
To continually strive for progress and to never belong,
To the status quo, but to strive for change,
And to always be willing to rearrange.

To always be aware of the bigger picture,
And to never let personal goals become a fixture,
But to always strive for team success,
And to always strive for the best.

To always be a valuable member,
And to always remember,
That every decision, position, and mistake,
It can have an impact, on the outcome, at stake.

So let us learn from the layoff,
And strive for growth, and never scoff,
With the need for change and progress,
In the end, it is the success that we must assess.

"The Journey of Continuous Growth and Improvement: A Poem on Embracing Change and Progress"

I can't stand still, for growth is my quest,
A decision I make each day to invest,
In knowledge, education, and new experiences,
To propel me forward to new frontiers and fences.

Change is a part of the growth process,
A push to new areas, geographies, and access,
To new perspectives, new ways of thinking,
A path to self-discovery and new beginnings.

Improvement is my desire to increase,
To discover new things, to innovate and release,
My talents, skills, and abilities,
To reach new heights, to achieve new possibilities.

Growth and improvement lead the way,
To self-sufficiency and a brighter day,
A cycle of continuous development, to extend,
To new directions across global and domestic trends.

So let me embrace them both,
Growth and improvement, my guiding oath,
For they are my best friends,
On my journey to success, until the very end.

"The Intertwining of Career and Passion: A Poem on Finding Harmony and Success"

Together they form a perfect blend,
Career and passion, till the very end,
One to provide for daily needs,
The other is to feed the soul, to plant the seeds.

With passion, the heart comes alive,
With a career, the mind thrives,
They both help me to grow,
To reach new heights, to know.

With passion, I can explore,
With my career, I can soar,
They both help me to find,
My purpose, my love, my grind.

With passion, I can create,
With my career, I can innovate,
They both help me to shine,
To be the best version of mine.

So let me embrace them both,
Career and passion, a perfect oath,
To work hard and to dream,
To live a life that's fulfilling.

"A Balance of Career and Passion: A Poem on Finding Harmony in Life and Work"

A balance of career and passion,
A path to earning and fashion,
An 8-hour day, a steady pace,
To ease financial worries, to keep up the race.

The work may be dull, the problems minor,
But I return each day to rise above it all,
My career is not just a job to sustain,
It's a growth path to progress, to gain.

Beyond the hours, it calls to me,
To push ahead, to be all I can be,
With focus and drive, I'll rise above,
And find new opportunities to explore and love.

My passion, too, is a driving force,
It brings change, creativity, and a different source of,
It reaches beyond income to build self-worth,
And allows my talents to flourish, explore, and birth.

So let them both intertwine,
Career and passion, a balance divine,
A path to earning, a way to growth,
A journey to self-discovery, to explore, to both.

"Rebuilding the Future: A Poem on Overcoming Setbacks and Embracing New Opportunities"

A new day dawns, the old one fades,
A chance to leave behind past mistakes,
With renewed strength and purpose true,
I'll build a future bright and new.

Though shadows loomed and doubts did creep in,
You gave me back my will to leap,
With an open heart and open mind,
I'll leave the past and doubts behind.

With talent, skills, and gifts in hand,
I'll take a stand and make a stand,
With integrity and honesty,
I'll chart my course to victory.

Through trials and hardships, I have grown,
And now my future's mine alone,
With hope and faith, I'll pave the way,
To brighter days, come what may.

So, here's to you, who gave me back,
The life I thought I'd lost, the track,
With gratitude and strength renewed,
I'll make a future bright and new.

"A Late-Night Call for Change: A Poem on Leadership, Community, and Giving"

They called her late one night,
With a request to make it right,
To lend her talent, time, and space,
To a cause, with purpose, to save face.

A list of leadership givers,
With insight into what it would take,
To recruit others like them,
To fight for a cause worth the stake.

The fight for women, children, and homes,
To end homelessness and to roam,
Freely, with dignity and pride,
With her limited living space, she decided to abide.

She provided the living space,
And soon found that her leadership gave pace,
Increased based on the cases she heard,
And the organization's workings that stirred.

Her living room and administration,
It gave her skills and abilities, a foundation,
In the end, her returns were more,
Then her time, talent, and financial score.

The reward increased her living space,
And her awareness of the community's plight,
A new perspective, a new point of view,
A cause worth fighting for and pursuing.

"The Journey of Growth and Purpose"

Her living space is now filled with purpose,
A cause worth fighting for, no one could coerce,
She became a leader, a giver of time,
And her talent, she used to climb.

To the top of the ladder of change and progress,
To help those in need with no regrets or stress,
She improved her community, one step at a time,
And her leadership abilities began to shine.

She became an inspiration to many,
A role model, with no need for any,
Fancy titles or awards, just a heart of gold,
And a will to make a difference, so bold.

Her living space is now filled with meaning,
A cause worth fighting for, with no learning,
Towards anything else, just a desire to help,
And to make a difference in the lives of yelp.

So let us all follow her lead,
And let our living space be filled with a need,
To help others and make a change,
For it is in giving that we genuinely arrange.

"The Journey of Becoming a Better Leader."

Becoming a better leader is a journey to take,
A path of growth, a decision to make,
To understand proper leadership behaviors,
And to watch our words and when we speak to our favors.

To watch the people, we spend our free time with,
And to understand the dynamics of each one.
To do what is right, even if it is unpopular,
And to always strive to be an example and a role model.

To know when to coach, mentor, and model,
And to know when to change and communicate the new vision and possible strategies.
To check our priorities every day,
And to ensure proper guidance in care is given in every way.

Becoming a better leader, a responsibility,
One that we must always take seriously,
For the people entrusted to our care,
Deserve our best, and we must always be aware.

So let us strive to be the best leader we can be,
And to lead with integrity and humility,
In the end, it is the people we serve,
That will determine our success and our worth.

"Stepping Back to Win: A Journey of Growth and Renewal"

I stepped back to win,
To gain new ground, to begin,
A journey of self-discovery,
And a path to true victory.

I stepped back, but I never fell,
I kept moving, and I stood tall,
With renewed strength and purpose true,
I forged ahead with a vision anew.

Though shadows loomed and doubts did creep in,
I knew that I had what it took to leap,
With an open heart and open mind,
I left the past and doubts behind.

With talent, skills, and gifts in hand,
I took a stand and made a stand,
With integrity and honesty,
I charted my course to victory.

Through trials and hardships, I have grown,
And now my future's mine alone,
With hope and faith, I'll pave the way,
To brighter days, come what may.

So, here's to me, who stepped back to win,
Who found new strength and a new way to spin,
With gratitude and strength renewed,
I'll make a future bright and new.

"It's Time to Go"

It's time to go; the clock is ticking,
The headache is throbbing; my mind is kicking,
The thought of work, another day,
The same old questions, what can I say?

Another meeting, with no progress made,
The office a prison, my spirit frayed,
Voices of people once admired,
Now cause of sweat, my appetite expired.

Fudging the truth for an egotist's gain,
My stomach churns, my mind in pain,
Painkillers, to ease the ache,
But it's time to stop this cycle from breaking.

The bills, the kids, college ahead,
The weight of it all, my mind is shed,
The ulcers, blood pressure, addictions too,
It's time to go; my path is valid.

It's time to leave this madness behind,
To find a new path, a new peace of mind,
It's not easy, but it's time to go,
And take control of my life, to know.

"Breaking Free"

The clock ticks on as I lay in bed,
My mind races with thoughts of dread,
Another day, in the rat race,
A cycle of stress with no escape.

The headache persists, a constant pain,
A reminder of the stress and strain,
Of working for a company, not my own,
Of being a pawn in a game unknown.

The thought of meetings with no progress,
A waste of time and a tremendous oppression,
The voices of colleagues once admired,
Now grating and causing me to tire.

The truth is fudged for the sake of gain,
A moral compromise, causing me disdain,
The bills and the kids, a constant worry,
A weight on my shoulders, in a hurry.

But now, it's time to take control,
To break free from the corporate mold,
It's time to go and find my way,
To a life with less stress and more play.

"Help Wanted: A Leader in Demand"

A leader in demand with a heart of gold,
A dedication to his team, his story to be told,
Enthusiastic and concerned for their well-being,
He has a proper level of intelligence for the business he's leading.

Bold and dynamic, when called to inspire,
Sacrifices made, with no room for tire,
Endurance for hours of interactions,
With government officials, stakeholders, and staff relations.

A strong communication vernacular, to be heard,
Emotionally aware, with the right words,
Presenting himself in an attractive package,
Ensuring his outfits are complementary to manage.

Always prepared to take on challenges,
Of an enthusiastic, motivated leader, he manages,
Emotionally stable, with financial awareness,
A leader who motivates, with moral ethics, in his harness.

Help wanted, a leader with these traits,
To guide and inspire, with no room for hate and no hate to create.

"The Search for a Leader"

A leader we need, with dedication and heart,
To guide us through challenges and set us apart,
With intelligence and boldness, he'll lead the way,
And inspire us to greatness, come what may.

He'll sacrifice for his team and the cause,
And endure the long hours without a pause,
He'll communicate with clarity and with care,
And always be aware of who's in the chair.

He'll present himself well, with style and class,
And always be prepared for each task,
He'll be emotionally stable and financially sound,
And lead with integrity, without a bound.

A leader we need, with vision and drive,
To motivate and inspire, to help us thrive,
With ethics and morals as his guiding light,
He'll lead us to success day and night.

So let us search, and let us find,
A leader of this caliber, one of a kind,
With dedication, intelligence, and heart,
He'll guide us to greatness and set us apart.

"The Mad Race for Success"

Are you madding enough yet, to join the race,
To strive for success, with a steady pace,
To go back to school and gain new skills,
To move your career to the next hills.

Do you need more time for training and growth,
To acquire expertise and knowledge to boast,
To seek the advice of a mentor or coach,
To reset your priorities and set a new approach.

Are you madding enough yet, to dress your product,
To maximize your talents and be in the market,
To act on faith, with integrity and respect,
To strive for your personal best and to not neglect.

So, join the mad race for success and fame,
For personal growth and to claim your name,
For a brighter future and a path to victory,
As you forget your way to win and to be free.

"The Road to Success: A Prescription for Growth"

Are you mad enough yet, to leap,
To leave behind the comfort and the cheap,
To strive for more, to reach for the stars,
To push beyond the limits and the bars.

Are you ready for the journey ahead,
To gain the knowledge and the skills to lead,
To seek out mentors and guides along the way,
To pave the path for a brighter day.

Are you angry enough yet, to reset your priorities,
To gain the balance for your personal best,
To set your goals and plan,
To act and to take a stand.

Are you mad enough yet, to market your talents,
To dress your product and to maximize,
To act on faith, with integrity,
To strive for success with humility.
So let us be mad enough to strive for our best,
To take the road to success and pass the test,
To be courageous and to be bold,
To reach for the stars and to be told.

We made it; we succeeded; we're the new us,
With knowledge, skills, and talents to trust,
So let us continue the road to success,
The journey is long, but the reward is nothing less.

"Lost in the Shuffle" is a poem about adult students' challenges.

Lost in the shuffle, with no predetermined fate,
Adult student struggles with so much on their plate.
With work and family, and daily demands,
It takes much work to find time for academic plans.

But still, they persevere, with determination and drive,
To improve their future and thrive.
They juggle their responsibilities with grace and poise,
And in the end, they make a choice.

To pursue their education, despite the challenges they face,
For a better future and a better place.
For adult students, the road may be extended,
But with persistence, they will prove they belong.

In the world of education, they'll make their mark,
And show that there is always time to embark.
So, let's support the adult student and help them succeed,
For a brighter future for all in need.

Adult students are an essential part of our society,
They are the ones who will shape the future with their diversity.

"Entrepreneurial Drive" Lesson from Thomas Edison

In the dark of night,
A bright spark of light,
A brilliant mind,
With a vision so optimistic.

Thomas Edison,
An inventor so great,
With determination and drive,
He met every fate.

With a goal in his heart,
And a fire in his soul,
He worked day and night,
To make his dream whole.

Though failure was frequent,
And setbacks were many,
He never gave up,
On his quest for something plenty.

He showed us all,
With hard work and grit,
We, too, can achieve,
A success that will fit.

So let us take inspiration,
From Edison's entrepreneurial drive,
And never give up,
On the dreams, we strive.

Success is not the absence of failure,
But the ability to rise above,
And like Thomas Edison,
We, too, can make a difference with love.

"Trust In the Lord"

Trust in the Lord; it's the key to success,
It helps guide and inspire all that's in excess.
Of possibility and potential, and all that's true,
It helps us achieve our goals and all that's due.

But it's not always easy, and all that's in store,
There are challenges and all that's in the bore.
That can hinder and hamper all that's in a way,
Trust in the Lord; it can sway.

But He is always there, and all that's true,
He will guide and inspire, and all that's in due.
To our path and journey, and all that we take,
He will help us find our way and all that we make.

So, let's embrace trust in the Lord and all that it brings,
And use it to guide and inspire and all that it means.
To overcome challenges and all that's in a way,
And achieve our goals and all that's in play.

Trust in the Lord; it's a way to succeed,
It's a way to navigate all that's in the lead.
Of possibility and potential, and all that's true,
Let's embrace it all and all that we do.

"Embrace All That You Are"

Embrace, it's a word that means to take in,
To hold close and dear, and all that's in kin.

To the things that matter and all that's true,
It's a way to find our place and all that we do.

Embrace, it's a word that means to accept,
To welcome and honor all that's in we are.

To the things that shape us and all that we are,
It's a way to find our way and all that's far.

Embrace, it's a word that means to love,
To cherish and honor all that's above.

To the things that matter and all that we hope,
It's a way to find our purpose and all we cope with.

So, let's embrace all that it brings,
And use it to find our way and all that it means.

To the things that matter and all that we hope,
Let's embrace all that we do.

For it's a way to find our place, and all that's true,
Let's embrace all that we are.

"The Ups and Downs of a Career"

I started with such high hopes and dreams,
A career full of promise, it seemed.
I worked hard and learned all I could,
But the road was bumpy and sometimes rough.
There were highs and lows, twists and turns,
Sometimes I soared; sometimes, I crashed and burned.
But through it all, I kept on going,
Determined to make my mark and keep growing.
I learned from my mistakes and took each day as it came,
Trying to stay focused and avoid the blame.
I worked hard and made sacrifices too,
But it all paid off, I'm happy to say.
Now I'm on a new path, one that's bright and true,
And though there will always be ups and downs,
I'm grateful for the journey and the lessons I've learned,
And I'm excited to see where this road will take me next,
Through the highs and lows, the good times, and the tests.

"Giving Birth as a Career Woman"

I was a career woman, driven and ambitious,
Focused on my job was all that I wished for.
But then something happened that changed my life,
A little bundle of joy, a beautiful wife.
I was scared and nervous but also filled with joy,
As I counted down the days until I could employ
All the love and care that I had to give,
To this little person whom I wanted to live
A happy, healthy life is full of love and light.
The day finally arrived, and I knew I was ready,
To face the challenge of giving birth, steady.
I pushed, and I panted, and finally, she arrived,
A tiny, perfect person whom I loved and admired.
It was a moment of pure, unbridled joy,
Holding my baby close, my love and pride were a glowing toy.
I knew that my career would consistently be important to me,
But this little person would always be my priority.
I am a career woman and a mother too,
And I will do my best to see them both through.
I will work hard and love fiercely every single day,
And watch my little one grow and learn and play.

"Mindfulness and Career Success"

In the rush and hustle of the working day,
It's easy to lose sight of what's essential, to stray.
From the path of mindfulness, of living in the present,
But it's in these moments that our success is cemented.
When we focus on the task at hand,
We give it our all; we take a stand.
Against distractions and external noise,
We find clarity; we find poise.
And in this clarity, we find success,
We rise to the top, and we surpass.
All the obstacles that stood in our way,
We find the strength to conquer each day.
So let us not forget the power of mindfulness,
Amid all the chaos and busyness.
For it is in this state of presence and calm,
That we find the path to career success, a beautiful balm.

"Making Next Level Decisions in Your Career"

I stand at a crossroads, unsure of which way to go,
Do I stay where I am or take the next step and grow?
My career is important to me; it's a big part of who I am,
But the thought of change can be scary; it's a daunting exam.
On the one hand, there's comfort in the familiar, in the known,
But on the other hand, there's excitement in the unknown.
The opportunity to learn and grow, to stretch me and see,
What I'm truly capable of, what I can be.
But making this decision isn't easy; it takes courage and faith,
To let go of the familiar and embrace the next phase.
Of my career, of my life, with all its ups and downs,
But I know that I'm ready; I'll wear my crown.
I'll take the leap of faith and see where it leads,
I'll embrace the unknown and all that it deems.
For I know that I'm strong and I have what it takes,
To face whatever comes my way and all the mistakes.
So, I'll take a deep breath and make the next level decision,
With courage and faith, I'll make the proper incision.
Into my future, into my career, with all its twists and turns,
And I'll face it all gracefully as I navigate the ups and downs.

"Balancing It All"

I'm trying to balance it all; it's a never-ending task,

The demands of work and home, it's a daunting task.

There's always something that needs to be done,

And sometimes, it feels like the day has just begun.

I'm juggling it all, trying to keep it all together,

But sometimes, it feels like I'm barely holding on, like a feather.

In the wind, blown every which way,

Trying to keep up with it all; it's a full day.

But somehow, I manage to keep it all going,

Even when I'm tired and my energy is low, I still show.

Up for it all, ready to tackle each day,

Because I know that I can do it, come what may.

So I'll keep on going and keep on trying,

To balance it all, to keep everything flying.

I'll take it one day at a time and do my best,

To find the balance that works for me and take a rest.

When I need it to recharge and renew,

So that I can keep on going and make it through.

The ups and downs, the twists and turns,

And find the balance that works for me and helps me learn.

To navigate it all with grace and ease,

And find the balance that works for me and helps me find peace.

"Mental Health and Awareness"

Mental health, it's such a crucial part of,
Of our overall well-being, it touches the heart.
Of whom we are and how we navigate,
The ups and downs of life, and the twists and turns that wait.
Sometimes, life can be challenging, and it can take its toll,
Leaving us feeling drained and overwhelmed, with no control.
Over our thoughts and emotions, as they spin and swirl,
Leaving us feeling lost and alone in an endless whirl.
But it's important to remember that we're not alone in this,
And that there is help and support if we're willing to ask.
For it, and to reach out and share how we feel,
To break the stigma and let our emotions heal.
So, let's talk about mental health and raise awareness too,
About the importance of taking care of ourselves and being accurate.
To whom we arc and how we feel,
For it's only then that we can begin to heal.
And find the strength and courage to face each day,
With hope and resilience as we navigate our way.
Through the ups and downs, the twists and turns,
And find the balance that works for us and helps us learn.
To prioritize our mental health and take care of ourselves,
So that we can be our best and find happiness.

"Courage and Life"

Courage, it's such a powerful thing,
It gives us the strength to face each day and to sing.
A song of hope and resilience, of strength and grace,
As we navigate the ups and downs and find our place.
In this world, which can be challenging and filled with strife,
But with courage, we can find the light and live our life.
To the fullest, and make the most of each day,
As we embrace the unknown and find our way.
Life is full of twists and turns, highs and lows,
But with courage, we can face them all and find the way to go.
Forward, with hope and grace, and find the strength to persevere,
Through all the challenges that come our way, and to live with cheer.
So let us embrace courage and all that it brings,
And use it to face each day and spread our wings.
To fly high and reach for the sky,
And find the strength to navigate it all and never say goodbye.
To our dreams and life, we want to live,
We can do it all with courage and be free to give.
Our all, and find the happiness we seek,
As we embrace courage and all that it means.

"The Country Life"

In the city, it's gone, goes, goes,
But in the country, it's time to take it slow.
To breathe in the fresh air and take in the sights,
To listen to the birds and feel the sun's warm light.
To wander through the fields and smell the sweet grass,
To stop and admire the flowers and watch the bees pass.
From blossom to blossom, as they gather their share,
Of the nectar and pollen that's found everywhere.
To take time to smell the roses and breathe in their scent,
To feel the cool breeze and be content.
Now, and be,
To find peace and tranquility and let go of the city.
In the country, it's easy to escape,
The hustle and bustle, the never-ending race.
To slow down and enjoy life and all that it brings,
Take time to smell the roses and the sweet honey suckle rings.
So, let's head to the country and take a break,
From the city's fast pace and all that it takes.
To find peace and calm, and just be,
And take time to smell the roses and all that we see.

"Love and Possibility"

Love, it's a powerful force that fills our hearts,
With hope and joy and a brand-new start.
It opens possibilities and helps us see,
All the beauty and wonder that life must be.
It gives us the strength to face each day,
With optimism and grace, as we find our way.
Through the ups and downs, the twists and turns,
And embrace all the love and possibility that love must learn.
For when we are in love, anything is possible,
We can conquer the world and find a new place to dwell.
In a world of hope and possibility,
Where anything is possible, and all is well.
So, let's embrace love and all that it brings,
And let it fill our hearts and help us find our wings.
To fly high and reach for the sky,
And embrace all the love and possibility that life has in store, oh my!
When we are in love and open to possibilities,
We can find happiness and joy and a sense of serenity.
So, let's embrace love and all that it brings,
And find the happiness and possibility that our hearts and soul sing.

"The Power of Social Currency"

Friendship, it's a special bond,
That keeps us connected and helps us find our way.
Through the ups and downs, the twists and turns,
It's a bond that helps us learn.
To love and be loved, and to support and encourage,
To lift each other and help each other flourish.
In this world that can be tough and full of strife,
Friendship helps us find the light and live our life.
To the fullest, and make the most of each day,
As we navigate the ups and downs and find our way.
Through the challenges that come our way, and find the strength to persevere,
Through all the ups and downs, live with cheer.
So, let's embrace friendship and all that it brings,
And use it to face each day and spread our wings.
To fly high and reach for the sky,
And find the strength to navigate it all and never say goodbye.
To our dreams and the life we want to live,
With friendship, we can do it all and be free to give.
Our all, and find the happiness we seek,
As we embrace friendship and all that it means.

"My Social Currency"

Social currency, it's a powerful force,
That can help us reach our goals and stay on course.
As we navigate this world and all that it brings,
It's the connections and relationships that help us spread our wings.
When we have a solid social currency, we have the power,
To tap into networks and resources, and find the support we need, every hour.
To achieve our goals and make the most of our time,
To build connections and relationships that are truly divine.
But it's not just about networking and connections,
It's about building genuine relationships and finding standard connections.
That goes beyond just surface level and truly matters,
For is these relationships that can help us climb the ladder.
So, let's cultivate our social currency and all that it brings,
And use it to reach our goals and spread our wings.
To fly high and achieve all that we desire,
And find the support and connections that help us rise higher.
The power of the social currency is a force to be reckoned with,
It can help us achieve our goals and make a difference without a glitch.
So, let's embrace it and all that it means,
And find the power and potential that our social currency beams.

"Handsel"

A handsel, it's a symbol of goodwill,
A gesture of good luck and a wish that's heartfelt.
It's a way to express our hopes and dreams,
And to share our good fortune, it gleams.
It's a way to inaugurate and mark a new beginning,
To start fresh and find the path that's winning.
To achieve our goals and make the most of our time,
To embrace the future and all that it brings with a chime.
For a handsel is more than just a gift,
It's a gesture of love and a wish that uplifts.
Our spirits and our hearts, and helps us find our way,
Through the ups and downs and all that we face.
So, let's embrace the handsel and all that it means,
And use it to mark new beginnings and all that gleams.
With hope and possibility and a sense of joy,
As we navigate this life and all that, it brings with our new toy.

"The Gourmand"

A new year's poem on gourmand describes someone who takes great pleasure in consuming great food and drinks.

As the New Year begins and a new chapter unfolds,
We look back on the past and all that we've been told.
About the joys of life and the pleasures it brings,
Like the love of good food and drink and all that it means.
For we are all gourmands, in our way,
We take pleasure in consuming all that we say.
About the joys of life and all that it holds,
We embrace the pleasures and all that it molds.
Into our lives and all that we are,
We revel in the tastes and textures and all that's far.
From mundane and ordinary and all that's dull,
We seek out the pleasures and all that's full.
Of flavor and delight, and all that's true,
We are gourmands, and all that we do.
Is seek out the pleasures and all that's grand,
We embrace the joys of life and all that's in hand.
So let's raise a glass and toast to the New Year,
And all that it brings, and all that's dear.
To us and all that we are,
We are gourmands, and all that's in store.
For the joys of life and all that it means,
We embrace the pleasures and all that gleam.
As we navigate this life and all that it brings,
We are gourmands and all that it means.

"The Skillful, Cunning, and Inventive One"

Daedal, it's a word that describes,
A skillful, cunning, or inventive other.
One who is adept at their craft,
And can create and innovate with their staff.
Of knowledge and expertise they wield,
To create and design with skill and speed.
They are masters of their art and all that it means,
To be daedal, and all that it entails.
For they possess a keen eye and a sharp mind,
They see the world in a different light and all that's designed.
To be creative and innovative, and all that's true,
They are daedal, and all that they do.
It is filled with skill and cunning and all that's grand,
They embrace their art and all that's in hand.
To create and innovate, and all that's meant,
They are daedal, and all that's spent.
On their craft and all that they do,
They are masters, and all that's true.
So, let's celebrate the daedal and all that they bring,
To the world, and all they are, and all they sing.

"Organization and Its Importance"

Organization, it's the key to success,
It helps us manage our time and all that we possess.
It keeps us on track and helps us stay focused,
It helps us achieve our goals and all that's enclosed.
In our lives and all that we do,
It helps us navigate the ups and downs, and all that's true.
To us and all that we are,
It helps us find balance and all that's far.
From chaos and clutter and all that's disorganized,
It helps us find order and all that's recognized.
As essential to our well-being,
It helps us find calm and all that's freeing.
So, let's embrace organization and all that it brings,
To our lives and all that it means.
To find balance and order, and all that's true,
We need organization and all that it does.
For it's a key to success and all that it entails,
We need organization and all that it entails.
To navigate this life and all that it brings,
We need organization and all that it means.

"Procrastination and Its Impact"

Procrastination, it's a habit we all know,
It creeps up on us and all that we show.
Of our best intentions and all that we plan,
It gets in the way and all that we stand.
For it's a habit that's hard to break,
It delays and puts off all that we make.
Of our goals and plans and all that we do,
It gets in the way, and all that's true.
To our well-being and all that we are,
It delays and puts off, and all that's far.
From our goals and plans and all that we seek,
It gets in the way, and all that's unique.
To our lives and all that we do,
It delays and puts off, and all that's true.
To our schoolwork and career, and all that we strive for,
It gets in the way, and all that's alive.
So, let's embrace the habit of procrastination,
And all that it means, and all that's in imagination.
And find the strength and courage to overcome,
This habit delays and puts off all that's done.
To our well-being and all that we are,
And find the strength and courage to go far.
And achieve our goals and all that we seek,
And find the balance and all that's unique

"The Power of Positive Thoughts"

Positive thoughts, they're a powerful force,
They can change our lives, and all that's, of course.
They have the power to shape our reality,
And bring us joy and all that's finality.
They help us find the light in times of darkness,
They give us hope and all that's holiness.
They help us see the good in all that isn't good,
They help us find the strength to be glad.
Positive thoughts have the power to change,
Our perspective and outlook, and all that's strange.
They help us see the world in a different light,
They help us find joy and all that's right.
So, let's embrace positive thoughts and all that they bring,
And use them to shape our reality and all that they sing.
Of hope and joy, and all that's true,
Let's fill our hearts and minds with positive thoughts and all that's new.
For they have the power to change our lives,
They can help us thrive.
So, let's embrace positive thoughts and all that they mean,
And let them guide us to all that's keen.

"Celebrating the New Year"

Variation, it's a time to celebrate,
The start of a new year and all that's great.
It's a time to reflect on all that's passed,
And look forward to all that's meant to last.
It's a time to set goals, and make resolutions,
To strive for success and all that's in fusion.
With our plans and dreams and all that we hope,
To achieve and accomplish all that, we cope.
With the challenges that come our way,
And embrace the new year and all that it says.
About the possibilities and all that's in store,
It's a time to celebrate and all that's more.
So, let's embrace variation and all that it brings,
And use it to celebrate, and all that rings.
Of hope and possibility, and all that's true,
Let's celebrate the new year and all that's new.

"Time Management"

Time management, it's the key to success,
It helps us stay on track and all that we express.
Of our goals and plans and all that we do,
It helps us navigate, and all that's true.
To our lives and all that we are,
It helps us find balance and all that's far.
From chaos and clutter and all that's disorganized,
It helps us find order and all that's recognized.
As important and necessary to our well-being,
It helps us find calm and all that's freeing.
It helps us achieve our goals and make the most of our time,
It helps us navigate all that's in line.
With our plans and dreams and all that we hope,
It helps us stay on track and all that we cope with.
With the challenges that come our way,
It helps us navigate all that's in play.
So, let's embrace time management and all that it brings,
To our lives and all that it means.
To find balance and order, and all that's true,
We need time management and all that it does.
For it's the key to success and all that it entails,
We need time management and all that it entails.
To navigate this life and all that it brings,
We need time management and all that it means.

"Life and Change"

Change, it's a constant in life,
But the pandemic brought it in a whole new light.
It changed how we work and all that we do,
It changed how we are educated, and all that's true.
To our lives and all that we are,
It changed our routines and all that far.
From what we knew before and all that was familiar,
It changed our world and all that's singular.
It forced us to adapt and find new ways,
To navigate this world and all that it says.
About the power of change and all that it means,
It forced us to embrace it, and all that gleams.
With possibility and hope, and all that's true,
It forced us to find new ways and all that's new.
To live and work, and all that we do,
It changed our world, and all that's true.
So, let's embrace change and all that it brings,
And use it to find new ways and all that rings.
Of hope and possibility, and all that's true,
Let's embrace change and all that's new.

"What is this, Job, Career, or Passion?"

A job, it's something we do to earn a living,
It helps us pay the bills and all that's given.
But a career, it's something more,
It's a path we choose and all that's in store.
It's a way to grow and all that we are,
It's a way to achieve and all that's far.
From just a job and all that it means,
A career is a journey, and all that gleams.
With possibility and potential, and all that's true,
A career is a path and all that's new.
It's a way to find meaning and all that's true,
It's a way to find purpose and all that's due.
But passion, it's something even more profound,
It's a fire that burns, and all that's a sweeper.
It's a calling, and all that's true,
It's a way to find joy and all that's due.
So, let's embrace these differences and all that they bring,
A job, a career, passion, and all that they sing.
Of purpose and meaning, and all that's true,
Let's embrace these differences and all that we do.

"Quiet Quitting"

Sometimes the noise becomes too much,
And all the striving, just out of touch.
The pressure mounts, the stress grows,
And we need to remember to follow our flows.
We're told never to give up, always to strive,
To push through and stay alive.
But sometimes, the bravest thing we can do,
It is to walk away and start anew.
Quiet quitting, it's not a sign of defeat,
It's a choice to take a seat.
To prioritize our well-being,
And let go of what's not worth seeing.
We're not giving up; we're not giving in,
We're just choosing a new beginning.
A chance to find a better way,
To live our lives day by day.
So, let's embrace the power of quiet quitting,
And see where it takes us, bit by bit.
It's a chance to let go and start anew,
And find the peace that's meant for you.

"Signs of Quiet Quitting"

Cynicism in their words and their eyes,
A disengaged team with a bit of surprise.
Projects unfinished, or low quality at best,
Expectations could be more precise, and communication could be better.
Overworked and micromanaged,
Growth opportunities are damaged.
Arriving late, leaving early, or sick days at will,
No interest in new skills or learning to fulfill.
Conflicts and tension, targets missed,
A team that was once thriving is now dismissed.
No initiative or ideas; they've checked out,
Participation and feedback, there's no shout.
Signs of quiet quitting it's plain to see,
A lack of motivation and a team in jeopardy.
Act and address the underlying pain,
Or risk losing your team to quiet disdain.
Open communication, feedback, and support,
It can keep your team motivated, and their efforts sustained.
Recognize the signs of quit quitting; it's true,
And work together to build a team that's renewed.

"My Best friends"

Growth and improvement, they're our best friends,
They help us achieve our goals, which are in a blend.
With our plans and dreams and all that we hope,
They help us navigate all that's in scope.
For growth and improvement, they're always there,
To guide and support, and all that's fair.
They help us find our way, and all that's true,
They help us achieve our goals and all that's new.
They help us find the strength and all that's meant,
To overcome challenges and all that's bent.
On our path to success, and in all that we do,
They help us navigate, and all that's true.
So, let's embrace growth and improvement and all that they bring,
And use them to achieve our goals and all that they sing.
Of possibility and potential, and all that's true,
Let's embrace growth and improvement and all that we do.
For they are our best friends and all that they mean,
They help us navigate, and all that's keen.
On our journey through life and all that it brings,
They're our best friends, and all it means is growth and improvement.

"Bad Bosses"

The lousy manager they're a thorn in our side,
They hinder and hamper all that we pride.
In our work and achievements, and all that we do,
They make it hard to succeed, and all that's true.
They micromanage and criticize, and all that's in the bore,
They undermine and discourage all that's in store.
To our confidence and motivation, and all that we are,
They make it hard to thrive, and all that's in a jar.
But we don't have to let them win, and all that's in scope,
We can find ways to rise above, and all that's in hope.
We can find ways to succeed, and all that's true,
We can find ways to thrive, despite a lousy manager and all we do.
So, let's embrace our strengths and all that they bring,
And use them to overcome all that they sing.
Of possibility and potential, and all that's true,
Let's rise above a lousy manager and all that we do.

"Quiet Firing"

Laid off, it's a word that brings fear,
It's a word that shakes us, and all that's clear.
To our foundations and all that we are,
It's a word those changes, and all that's far.
From our plans and dreams and all that we hoped,
It's a word for those challenges and all that's imposed.
On our sense of security, and all that's true,
It's a word that shakes us and all that's due.
But it's also a word that brings opportunity,
It's a word that forces us to find new ways and all that's in unity.
To navigate this world and all that it means,
It's a word that forces us to embrace change and all that gleams.
With possibility and hope, and all that's true,
It's a word that forces us to find new ways and all that's new.
To live and work, and all that we do,
It's a word those changes, and all that's true.
So, let's embrace the word "laid off" and all that it brings,
And use it to find new ways and all that rings.
Of hope and possibility, and all that's true,
Let's embrace "laid off," and all that's new.

"True Profit Killers"

The ineffective leader, they're a burden to bear,
They hinder and hamper, and all that's unfair.
To our growth and success, and all that we hope,
They need help to achieve all that's in scope.
They lack vision and direction, and all that's in the bore,
They need to inspire and guide all that's in store.
To our ambition and motivation, and all that we are,
They make it hard to thrive, and all that's in a jar.
But we don't have to let them hold us back, and all that's in scope,
We can find ways to rise above, and all that's in hope.
We can find ways to succeed, and all that's true,
We can find ways to thrive, despite an ineffective leader and all we do.
So, let's embrace our strengths and all that they bring,
And use them to overcome all that they sing.
Of possibility and potential, and all that's true,
Let's rise above an ineffective leader and all that we do.

"The Power of PsyCap"

Resilience and perseverance, hope and self-efficacy,
They're the tools we need to navigate, and all that's in capacity.
The challenges and setbacks, and all that's in store,
They help us overcome all that's in the bore.
Resilience and perseverance, they're the strength we need,
To face and overcome all that's in the seed.
Of doubt and fear, and all that's in a way,
They help us find our footing and all that's in sway.
Hope and self-efficacy, they're the light we need,
To guide and inspire, and all that's in the lead.
To our goals and dreams, and all that we hope,
They help us navigate all that's in scope.
So, let's embrace resilience and perseverance, hope and self-efficacy,
And use them to overcome all that's in capacity.
The challenges and setbacks, and all that's in store,
Let's embrace these tools, all we do, and all that's in the weary.

"Team Morale"

Building good morale, it's the key to success,
It helps boost and motivate all that's in excess.
Of possibility and potential, and all that's true,
It helps us achieve our goals and all that's due.
But it's not always easy, and all that's in store,
There are challenges and all that's in the bore.
That can hinder and hamper all that's in a way,
Building good morale can sway.
The effectiveness of a team and all that it means,
Building good morale can gleam.
With positivity and hope, and all that's true,
It helps us navigate all that's new.
So, let's embrace building good morale and all that it brings,
And use it to boost and motivate and all that it means.
To overcome challenges and all that's in a way,
And achieve team effectiveness and all that's in play.
Building good morale, it's a way to succeed,
It's a way to navigate all that's in the lead.
Of possibility and potential, and all that's true,
Let's embrace it all and all that we do.

"Set Back for Come Back"

Thank you for giving me back my life,
For allowing me to explore opportunities and all that's rife.
With possibility and potential, and all that's true,
Thank you for giving me back my life; all that's new.
I never thought it was possible, in this crazy world of setbacks,
But you opened doors, and all that's intact.
To my talents and skills, and all that I am,
You gave me a chance to explore and expand.
On my journey through life and all that it brings,
You gave me back my life and all that it means.
To find my purpose and all that's true,
You gave me back my life and all that's new.
So, thank you for giving me back my life,
For all that you've done and all that's rife.
With possibility and potential, and all that's true,
Thank you for giving me back my life and all that I do.

"Leadership, Fallacies, and Organizational Effectiveness"

Leadership, it's the key to success,
It helps guide and inspire all that's in excess.
Of possibility and potential, and all that's true,
It helps us achieve our goals and all that's due.
But it's not always easy, and all that's in store,
There are fallacies and all that's in the bore.
That can hinder and hamper all that's in a way,
Leadership and fallacies can sway.
The effectiveness of an organization and all that it means,
Leadership and fallacies can lean.
On each other and all that's in store,
To shape and influence, and all that's in the bore.
So, let's embrace leadership and all that it brings,
And use it to guide and inspire and all that it means.
To overcome fallacies and all that's in a way,
And achieve organizational effectiveness and all that's in play.
For leadership, fallacies, and organizational effectiveness,
They're all connected, and all that's in excess.
Of possibility and potential, and all that's true,
Let's embrace them all and all that we do.

"Leadership Givers"

They called her late one night,
Based on a list of leadership givers and all that's in sight.
Who might have some insight on what it would take,
To recruit others like them, and all that's at stake.
To continue the fight, the fight for a worthwhile cause,
They needed guidance, and all that was in pause.
To find their way, and all that's true,
They turned to her and all that was due.
For she was a leader, and all that she meant,
She knew, and all that's in bent.
On helping others and all that she does,
She was a leader, and all that's true.
So, they called her late one night,
And asked for her help and all that was in sight.
To continue the fight, the fight for a worthwhile cause,
They needed her guidance, and all that was in pause.
And she was happy to oblige,
She knew, and all that's in size.
To help them find their way, and all that's true,
She was a leader, and all that she did.
So, they called her late one night,
And she answered the call, and all that was in sight.
To continue the fight, the fight for a worthwhile cause,
She was a leader, all she was, and all that's in pause.

"Stepping Back to Win at Life"

Stepping back, it's a hard thing to do,
It's a way to regroup, and all that's true.
To find our footing and all that's meant,
To navigate this thing called life and all that's sent.
With changes swift and all that's in the wind,
It can be hard to keep up, and all that's pinned.
To our plans and dreams and all that we hope,
It can be hard to navigate, and all that's in scope.
But stepping back it can help us see,
The bigger picture and all that's in be.
It can help us find our way, and all that's true,
It can help us navigate all that's due.
So let's embrace stepping back and all that it brings,
And use it to regroup and all that it means.
To find our footing, and all that's true,
Let's embrace stepping back and all that we do.
For it's a way to win this thing called life,
It's a way to navigate and all that's rife.
With changes swift and all that's in the wind,
Stepping back can help us win and all that's in kin.

"Managing My Career"

Managing my career, it's a way to achieve,
My dreams and goals, and all that I believe.
To be possible, and all that's true,
It's a way to navigate all that I do.
I've established specific goals based on my vision of me,
And I work towards them and all that I see.
As achievable, and all that's in store,
I work towards them and all that's in the bore.
For my career is my path, and all that I take,
It's a way to find my place and all that I make.
Of my life and all that I am,
It's a way to find purpose and all that I stand for.
So, I manage my career and all that I do,
To achieve my dreams and goals, and all that's true.
For they are essential, and all that I hold,
I manage my career to achieve them; all that's in the fold.

"Ready for Your Next Move"

Ready for your next move? It's a way to succeed,
It's a way to find your place and all that's in the lead.
To your goals and dreams and all that you hope,
It's a way to navigate all that you cope with.
With the challenges that come your way,
It's a way to find your footing and all that you say.
To your path and journey and all that you take,
It's a way to find your place and all that you make.
So be ready for your next move and all that it brings,
And use it to find your place and all that it means.
To your goals and dreams and all that you hope,
Be ready for your next move and all that you cope.
For it's a way to succeed, and all that you do,
Be ready for your next move, and all that's true.

Closing Remarks

This beautiful book of poems is the perfect keepsake for any graduate, with its timeless messages of hope, grit, and perseverance. Whether your loved one is embarking on a new career, heading off to college, or simply beginning a new chapter in their life, this book will be a source of inspiration and guidance for years to come. The book has aimed to provide a unique career and talent development perspective through poetry. We have explored the importance of social, political, intellectual, psychological, and human capital in today's job market. We have also delved into the importance of introspection and self-reflection in managing one's career and personal development.

This book of poems also celebrates the wisdom and inspiration of some of the greatest commencements while providing a keepsake treasure for your loved ones as they prepare to embark on the next chapter of their life. This book will inspire and guide them for years to come. The book of poems combines the best messages and themes from some of the most famous commencement speeches of our time, including David Foster Wallace's "This is Water," Steve Jobs's "Stay Hungry, Stay Foolish," and Chimamanda Ngozi Adichie's "We Should All Be Feminists."

As we end this book, we hope the poetry and introspection questions have inspired you to look deeper into your career and talent development. We encourage you to take the time to reflect on your own career goals, identify areas for improvement, and act toward achieving them.

It is important to remember that as the job market changes, it is up to everyone to take responsibility for their career development. The traditional models of company security and automatic career progression are becoming a thing of the past. It is up to each of us to build a talent portfolio that aligns with the skills and abilities required in today's job market.

We hope this book has given you the inspiration and tools to take control of your career development. Remember to reflect on your progress and adjust as required continually. We wish you all the best in your career journey and hope you continue striving for success and personal growth.

Best of luck,
Dr. Marilyn Carroll, Ph.D.
Mother, Writer, Researcher, Professor, Entrepreneur, Renaissance woman

Resources to Help You on Your Journey

Throughout this book of poems, on reflections of self-discovery, a poetic journey of introspection, we have covered many things from generations. How do generations in the workforce, the five generations, perceive work and life in their career and their communities to career perspectives and points that talk about that and give us pause for introspection and reflection? We have also covered how to look at various jobs from a poetic standpoint and how those all intertwined, so we hope you have enjoyed the book. We hope you can use some of the available resources we have included at the end of the book, and we'd like to know your thoughts, so contact us at the publisher or at the information we provide.

For Self-Reflection

I encourage you to reflect on your experiences and feelings related to the topics covered in the poems. Reflect on what you have read and how it relates to your life. These are also great questions to spark group conversation.

- What do you think is the biggest challenge facing the workforce today?

- How have your experiences with quitting a job shaped your views on work and career?

- What has been your experience working with colleagues from different generations?

- How have diversity and inclusion been addressed in your workplace?

- How do you feel about the culture of your current workplace?

- Are there any skills or talents that you have that you feel are undervalued in your current job?

- How do you think the current state of the job market and the economy affects job opportunities?

- What are your thoughts on the importance of work-life balance?

- How do you think the future of work will change, and what skills will be needed to succeed in the future workforce?

- How do you feel about the current state of the education system, and what do you think needs to be improved?

- How do you plan to grow and develop in your career?

Career Resources

1. **Online career management and development courses**: Websites such as Coursera, Udemy, and LinkedIn Learning offer a variety of methods for career management, networking, and resume writing.

2. **Career coaching**: Consider working with a career coach who can provide personalized guidance and support in developing your career plan.

3. **Networking events:** Attend local networking events and conferences to connect with professionals in your industry and expand your network.

4. **Professional associations:** Join a professional association related to your field to stay updated on industry trends and connect with other professionals.

5. **Job search websites:** Utilize online job search platforms such as LinkedIn and Glassdoor to explore job opportunities and research companies.

6. **Career development books and articles:** Read books and articles on career development, networking, and personal branding to gain new insights and strategies.

7. **LinkedIn Groups**: Join relevant LinkedIn groups to connect with professionals in your industry and stay updated on industry news and job opportunities.

8. **Online communities:** Join online communities like Reddit or Facebook groups focused on career development and networking to connect with like-minded professionals.

9. **Personal branding tools:** Utilize Canva, Grammarly, and Hootsuite to improve your branding and online presence.

10. **Career assessment tests:** Take online career assessment tests to gain insight into your interests, values, and strengths and to explore potential career options.

Suggested books to supplement the information in this book include:

1. *"The Talent Code" by* Daniel Coyle delves into the science of talent and skill development.

2. *"The 7 Habits of Highly Effective People"* by Stephen Covey offers practical personal and professional growth advice.

3. *"Drive The Surprising Truth About What Motivates Us"* by Daniel H. Pink explores the science of motivation and *how to tap into it.*

4. *"Outliers: The Story of Success"* by Malcolm Gladwell examines the factors contributing to success in various fields.

5. *"Mindset: The New Psychology of Success"* by Carol S. Dweck explores the power of a growth mindset in achieving success.

6. *"The Power of Intentional Leadership"* by John C. Maxwell focuses on developing leadership skills and inspiring others to achieve their goals.

7. *"Leadership and Self-Deception"* by the Arbinger Institute examines how self-deception can undermine leadership effectiveness.

8. *"The Art of Possibility"* by Rosamund Stone Zander and Benjamin Zander provides tools for expanding your vision of what is possible in your personal and professional life.

9. *"The Lean Startup"* by Eric Ries explores lean methodology principles and how they can be applied to startups and other organizations.

10. *"Start with Why"* by Simon Sinek examines the importance of understanding your purpose and how it can inspire others to succeed.

Career assessment tools for insight into your strengths, weaknesses, and areas for improvement.

Some popular career assessment tools include:

- the Myers-Briggs Type Indicator (MBTI),
- the Strong Interest Inventory, and
- the Holland Code

These assessments can help individuals understand their personality type, interests, and preferred work environment, which can aid in identifying potential career paths.

Another valuable resource is the O*NET database, which provides detailed information on different occupations, including skills, abilities, and interests required for success in those careers. Additionally, individuals can seek career counseling or coaching services to help them explore and identify their unique talents and passions, set goals, and create action plans to achieve their career aspirations.

Résumé Help

Résumé help can come in many forms, such as seeking advice from a career counselor or mentor, utilizing online resources such as résumé building websites or templates, or hiring a professional résumé writer. Some tips for creating an effective résumé include highlighting relevant skills and experience, using keywords, and tailoring the résumé to the specific job or industry. Additionally, it's essential to proofread and have someone else review the résumé for errors or areas of improvement. Other resources that could be helpful include attending résumé writing workshops or webinars or taking a class or course on résumé writing. It's also recommended to keep the résumé updated regularly and to tailor it to each job application.

Made in the USA
Columbia, SC
14 April 2023

15352965R00072